101 TIPS FOR MANDOLIN

CW00493146

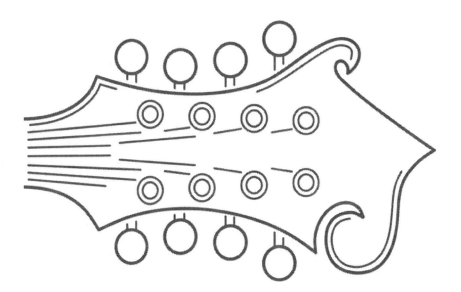

BY
PHILIP JOHN BERTHOUD

CONTENTS

Left hand...3
Chords/Right Hand 11
Practice.......................................19
Theory 25
Traditional Music.......................33
Improvisation 37
Posture 40
Instrument Care/Accessories....42
Miscellaneous............................46

The left-hand fingers are numbered:

Index finger – 1st finger
Middle finger – 2nd finger
Ring finger – 3rd finger
Little finger – 4th finger

The mandolin strings are numbered as follows:

1st	E	thinnest
2nd	A	
3rd	D	
4th	G	thickest

The strings are described singularly, even though they are in pairs.

---

* It has been assumed that the reader is right-handed. Therefore the fingering hand is referred to as the left hand, while the picking hand is the right hand. If you are left-handed, please adjust accordingly.

1

Keep unused left-hand fingers close to the fret-board, ready for use. Letting them drift away will cut down on your playing speed and fluency.

GOOD

BAD

2

When shifting to a higher position, for example moving from the second to twelfth fret, anticipate the move by focussing on the destination fret just before it is time to play it. By doing this, it is possible to stay one jump ahead, keeping you on top of the music and helping to make the overall sound more smooth and confident.

3

Pick up a sheet of newspaper and scrunch it up into a ball using only one hand. This will exercise the finger and hand muscles, and is particularly good for improving left-hand agility and strength.

4

Playing speed and fluency can be seriously hampered by gripping the neck of the mandolin too tightly. Aim to hold the neck loosely, in a relaxed way, only using pressure when and where required.

5

A general rule for left hand fingers is to use as little pressure as possible. This applies to solo playing and chord playing. Using the minimum pressure allows you to play faster and more fluidly. In order to find the minimum pressure required do the following:

- Place a finger on a particular note.
- Now release the pressure exerted by that finger so that it is just resting on the string.
- Now start picking the same string with the right hand. You should hear a dull, dampened sound.
- Keep picking it, while slowly increasing the pressure with the left hand finger. Eventually, you will start to hear a clear note emerge, assuming the finger is in the correct position. This will tell you the minimum pressure required.
- Now pick the note loudly, softly, slowly and quickly, all the time keeping the pressure constant.

The same exercise can be done with a chord shape.

If too much pressure is needed, your mandolin may not be properly set up. Take it to a repairer to get a professional opinion.

The hammer-on is shown in written music by a curved line known as a **slur**.

A hammer-on involves two notes, a lower sounding note followed by a higher sounding note. The first one is picked or plucked as normal, but the second is sounded by the left hand alone. By bringing the finger down forcibly at the desired fret, it is possible to make a note without picking or plucking the string. The example above shows four different hammer-ons. As you can see, the lower note can be open or fretted.

7

Pull-offs are very similar to hammer-ons, at least in theory. The difference is that the first note is higher. The example below shows four pull offs:

As with hammer-ons, the first is plucked or picked as normal, but the second note is played using the left hand alone. To do this, first pick the string and pull the higher note finger off the string sideways, in such a way that the string is "plucked" by the left hand. This will then make the lower note sound.

* Where the two notes are fretted notes, put both fingers down first, before picking the upper note.

Hammer-ons and pull-offs can be combined, as in the example below:

In each of the four examples above, there are three notes involved. The first is plucked, the second is hammered-on and the last is pulled-off. Of these three notes, only the first is sounded by the right hand.

* In the third example, the 2nd fret note will be held down for the duration of the hammer-on and pull-off.

Another common technique, also involving two notes linked by a curved line or slur, is the **slide**. The difference in notation is the straight line that extends from the first to second note.

In the above examples, the first note of each pair is plucked or picked as normal, but the second note is sounded by sliding the finger quickly along the string without taking off the pressure. This allows the string to keep vibrating and, with practice, a note will be clearly heard wherever the finger comes to rest.

Look at the three pictures below, all showing the left hand first finger playing B on the A string.

The reader may notice that an undesirable hand position is used in these photos (see tip 1). This is done to make viewing of the finger placement easier.

a)

A different part of the finger tip is being used in each picture:

In this picture the finger is placed centrally on the string.

b)

The next picture shows the finger closer to the E string, although it is still holding down the A string. The D string is left clear

c)

In the third picture the finger is nearer the D string, leaving the E string clear.

See tip 11

To illustrate tip 20 further, look at the music examples below.

In all of them, the B note is to be held down for the duration of the two bars.

Photo b) from tip 11 shows how to hold this B note for music examples 1 and 2, while photo c) corresponds with examples 3 and 4. This way of fingering is very useful for quick and smooth playing.

The little finger is often the weakest, so in order to
strengthen it, do exercises that focus on it. In the
exercises below the little finger notes are indicated by
the figure 4.

CHORDS/RIGHT HAND

As well as being a great melodic instrument, the mandolin is also highly effective when it comes to backing or accompanying.

If you are already a guitarist, as many mandolinists seem to be, it is simply a matter of learning some new chord shapes. A helpful similarity between the two instruments is that the mandolin is tuned G D A E (lowest sounding to highest sounding), the same as the lowest-sounding four strings of the guitar (in reverse). Because of this, many mandolin chord shapes look like reversed images of their guitar equivalents. For example compare the mandolin chords (above) with the guitar chords (below):

Mandolin chords:

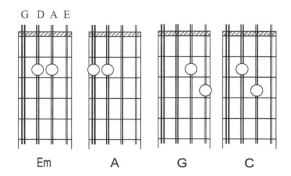

Guitar chords:

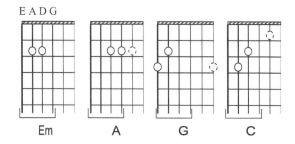

When strumming, it is common to keep the right hand moving up and down in regular time with the music, even if it is not coming into contact with the strings every time. In the example below, the hand movement is shown by arrows. Arrows with a solid head show where the strings are struck, and arrows with a hollow head show where the hand moves past the strings without coming into contact with them. This technique helps to keep the basic rhythm of the music solid.

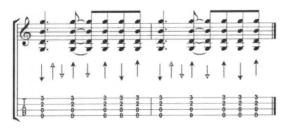

15

There are some great movable chord shapes available to the mandolin player. Below are shown A and E modal. Open strings are indicated by an "o", and unplayed strings with an "x"

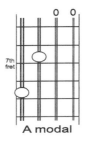 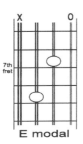

A modal   E modal

For both of these chords, the first finger is on the 7th fret and the second finger is on the 9th. Also try the same shapes in the positions shown in the chart below, still playing with the same open strings.

	1st finger on…	2nd finger on…
Chord 1	5th fret	7th fret
Chord 2	3rd fret	5th fret
Chord 3	2nd fret	4th fret
Chord 4	4th fret	6th fret

A or E modal followed by chords 1, 2 and 3 work well, as do A or E modal with chords 3 and 4. Try other combinations

16

When a single letter is used to denote a chord, this chord will be **major**. A is short for A major, C$\sharp$ is short for C$\sharp$ major, etc.

17

The note names on the 4th (G) string are shown on the chart below

Fret	Note name
Open	G
1st fret	G$\sharp$/A$\flat$
2nd fret	A
3rd fret	A$\sharp$/B$\flat$
4th fret	B
5th fret	C
6th fret	C$\sharp$/D$\flat$
7th fret	D
8th fret	D$\sharp$/E$\flat$
9th fret	E
10th fret	F
11th fret	F$\sharp$/G$\flat$
12th fret	G

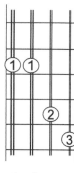

If you make a G-shape barre-chord (right) with the first finger on one of the frets as shown in this chart, the note name of that fret on the 4th string will give you the chord name. For example a G-shape barre-chord played with the first finger on the 5th fret will be a C chord. The same shape with the first finger on the 3rd fret will be a B$\flat$ or A$\sharp$ chord.

18

The note names on the 3rd (D) string are shown on the chart below

Fret	Note name
Open	D
1st fret	D$\sharp$/E$\flat$
2nd fret	E
3rd fret	F
4th fret	F$\sharp$/G$\flat$
5th fret	G
6th fret	G$\sharp$/A$\flat$
7th fret	A
8th fret	A$\sharp$/B$\flat$
9th fret	B
10th fret	C
11th fret	C$\sharp$/D$\flat$
12th fret	D

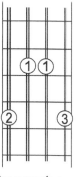

If you make a D-shape barre-chord (right) with the first finger on one of the frets as shown in this chart, the note name of that fret on the 3rd string will give you the chord name. For example a D-shape barre-chord played with the first finger on the 5th fret will be a G chord. The same shape with the first finger on the 3rd fret will be an F chord.

Variations on the movable G chord shapes can be found below.

Use the table, which shows the chords that can be found using these shapes.

F#, G# and C# can also be read as Gb, Ab and Db, respectively. Likewise Bb and Eb can be read as A# and D# *(see tip 46)*.

For the sake of completeness, examples are given right up to the 12th fret, although barre-chords are not normally practical this high.

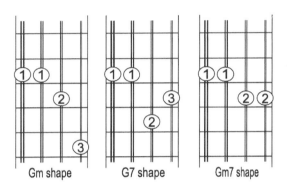

Gm shape   G7 shape   Gm7 shape

G shape barre/movable-chords				
fret for 1st finger	Chord from G shape barre-chord	Chord from Gm shape barre-chord	Chord from G7 shape barre-chord	Chord from Gm7 shape barre-chord
1	G#	G#m	G#7	G#m7
2	A	Am	A7	Am7
3	Bb	Bbm	Bb7	Bbm7
4	B	Bm	B7	Bm7
5	C	Cm	C7	Cm7
6	C#	C#m	C#7	C#m7
7	D	Dm	D7	Dm7
8	Eb	Ebm	Eb7	Ebm7
9	E	Em	E7	Em7
10	F	Fm	F7	Fm7
11	F#	F#m	F#7	F#m7
12	G	Gm	G7	Gm7

as shown
in tip 17

20

Variations on the movable D chord shapes can be found below.

Use the table, which shows the chords that can be found using these shapes.

F$\sharp$, G$\sharp$ and C$\sharp$ can also be read as G$\flat$, A$\flat$ and D$\flat$, respectively. Likewise B$\flat$ and E$\flat$ can be read as A$\sharp$ and D$\sharp$ *(see tip 46)*.

For the sake of completeness, examples are given right up to the 12th fret, although barre-chords are not normally practical this high.

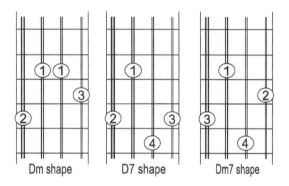

Dm shape   D7 shape   Dm7 shape

D shape barre/movable-chords				
fret for 1st finger	Chord from **D shape** barre-chord	Chord from **Dm shape** barre-chord	Chord from **D7 shape** barre-chord	Chord from **Dm7 shape** barre-chord
1	E$\flat$	E$\flat$m	E$\flat$7	E$\flat$m7
2	E	Em	E7	Em7
3	F	Fm	F7	Fm7
4	F$\sharp$	F$\sharp$m	F$\sharp$7	F$\sharp$m7
5	G	Gm	G7	Gm7
6	G$\sharp$	G$\sharp$m	G$\sharp$7	G$\sharp$m7
7	A	Am	A7	Am7
8	B$\flat$	B$\flat$m	B$\flat$7	B$\flat$m7
9	B	Bm	B7	Bm7
10	C	Cm	C7	Cm7
11	C$\sharp$	C$\sharp$m	C$\sharp$7	C$\sharp$m7
12	D	Dm	D7	Dm7

as shown
in tip 18

21

The left hand is effective for "damping", or cutting out the sound, on chords with no open strings, which is very useful for developing dynamic-sounding accompaniments:

- Play a chord with no open strings, so that all the notes are ringing out.

- Remove the pressure exerted by the left hand without losing contact with the strings.

- The sound will stop completely.

22

The left hand can be used to dampen open chords. Taking the chord of G as an example:

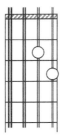

The first and second fingers are used to finger this chord. This leaves the third and fourth fingers free. Either can be used to dampen the sound of the strummed G chord by simply resting them across the vibrating strings, whilst still holding the chord down.

23

The picking hand can also be used for damping. This simply involves putting the hand on strings that are vibrating in order to stop them sounding. This can be useful for "open chords" (chords that contain open strings), as it is may be more awkward for the left hand to deal with the damping on these chords.

24

Things to look out for if chords are a problem:

- Is your left hand in the right position?

- Is enough pressure being exerted by
  the left-hand fingers? Don't give up if
  this is case. Difficulties are often due
  to the fact that the muscles involved in
  playing chords are not developed.
  Keep on practicing a little at a time and
  the strength will come as it does to any
  muscle that is exercised.

- Are the left-hand fingers getting in the
  way of strings other than those they
  should be holding down?

25

If learning a chord progression with awkward changes,
practice the changes silently, without using the right
hand. This allows you to fully concentrate on the left
hand without any distraction.

26

Although the pick will need to be gripped a little more
tightly when playing louder, it is advisable, at all times,
to hold it only tight enough to stop it falling from your
hand.

27

When strumming, it is not necessary to hold the
plectrum too tightly or to hold the fingers too rigidly.
Try strumming with a lighter touch, imagine brushing
the strings, rather than striking them.

28

It is necessary for the wrist to be supple at all times.
This is especially important when playing fast.
Stiffness in the wrist will slow you down and create
tension and discomfort.

29

Make friends with scales – run through a few each time you practice. There really is no better way to improve playing accuracy and knowledge of the mandolin. If you are not sure what to do and/or can't find a book of mandolin scales, look at a book of violin scales, which will contain the same notes and fingerings.

30

Plan your practice sessions. Here is a possible format for a 1 hour practice:

Tune up	
Warm up with scales/exercises	5 mins
Warm up with chord progressions	5 mins
Run through tune or chord progression to practice	5 mins
Play through again, slowly, identifying any problem areas	10 mins
Isolate problem areas, analyse difficulties and ascertain what work needs to be done – change of fingering, change in picking, etc	15mins
Play through tune or chord progression again, this time with alterations made	5 mins
Play through some other pieces that you know well and enjoy.	15 mins

Make your own timetable, better suited to your own needs and timescale.

31

If you are learning a piece of music, it can be
frustrating if there is one bit that always bugs you
because it's too difficult. Ascertain which group of
notes is causing the problem and play them over and
over again slowly, creating a useful exercise in the
process. For example:

32

The word "practice" can be interpreted in a negative
way. Thinking of it as "focussed playing" is more
positive. "*Focussed*" because it is a time to look more
closely at what you can and can't do. "*Playing*"
because you are playing music, even when you practice
– the element of enjoyment should not be forgotten.

The best musicians are those that relish any opportunity
to play, whether focussed on practicing or performing.

33

For a variation on the usual scales, try altering the order
of the scale notes. For example, see the different ways
of playing the D major scale below. This will improve
finger independence.

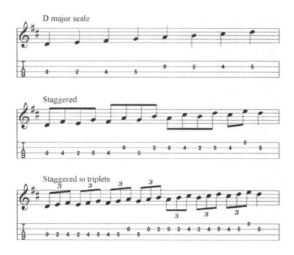

34

Try playing scales without using open notes, in order to
strengthen the fingers, especially the little finger. The
example below is the same as above, with the open
notes replaced by 7th fret notes.

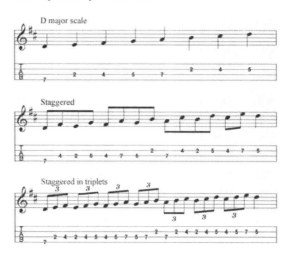

22

35

If a tune/technique/chord progression is causing difficulties take the tune or isolate the difficult section and play it much more slowly. Slowing down the tempo allows you to really look closely at what's happening, seeing your playing through a magnifying glass. This puts you in a better position to rectify the problem.

36

When practicing scales, it can be useful to say the names of the notes out loud to help familiarise yourself with the location of different notes up and down the fretboard.

37

In order to get the "feel" of the instrument, without relying too much on looking, spend some practice time playing without looking at the hands, getting used to *feel* of the fingerboard and strings. When it comes to playing an instrument, the sense of touch is far more sensitive and accurate than sight.

For those who haven't played long, this may be quite demanding, but potentially very rewarding. For the more advanced player, pieces of music that involve a lot of moving up and down the fretboard will be more appropriate for this exercise.

38

Practice time is a great opportunity to work on difficult pieces, ironing out problem areas and concentrating on improving technique. However, it is also great to play music you know really well and enjoy the fact that it sounds good.

Practice doesn't always have to be hard work.

Aim to introduce at least one new variation to a tune each time you practice. This could include playing more than one string or an alteration in the melody. See the examples below – first play melody 1, then try out the two possible variations. Then do the same with melody 2:

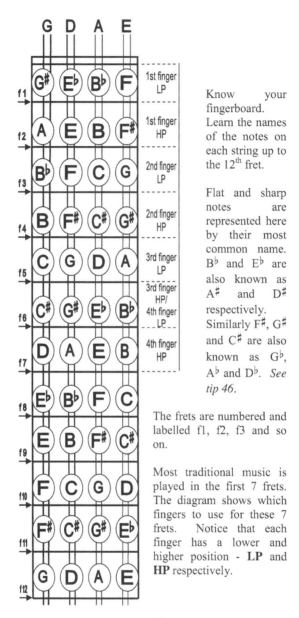

Know your fingerboard. Learn the names of the notes on each string up to the 12th fret.

Flat and sharp notes are represented here by their most common name. B♭ and E♭ are also known as A♯ and D♯ respectively. Similarly F♯, G♯ and C♯ are also known as G♭, A♭ and D♭. *See tip 46.*

The frets are numbered and labelled f1, f2, f3 and so on.

Most traditional music is played in the first 7 frets. The diagram shows which fingers to use for these 7 frets. Notice that each finger has a lower and higher position - **LP** and **HP** respectively.

The higher position for the 3rd finger is the same as the lower position for the 4th finger. As a general rule, the third finger will be used in this case if the music you are playing shows the note as sharp (♯), and the 4th finger will be used if it is flat (♭).

41

If you learn a tune from written music put away the music sheet/book as soon as you've committed it to memory, and don't go back to it unless you really have to.

42

The pairs of strings on the mandolin are tuned the same as the strings on a violin, so music for the latter is very often suitable for the former.

43

While much can be picked up from mandolin tab, a lot more information can be conveyed in standard notation (or the dots). A versatile mandolinist will be at ease with both forms of notation.

44

If you play traditional styles on the mandolin and learn your tunes from written music, then beware. Over reliance on the printed music can make your music seem lifeless. Always be open to experimentation and variation within the basic structure of the tune.

45

It is not vital to be able to read music in order to play traditional music. However, it can be extremely useful if you are quite new to a particular style. For someone who has grown up with traditional music around them, it will be easier to pick up the style as the sound will already be a part of them. If you are quite new to the style you want to learn, a lot of listening and extra work will be needed. Once you are more familiar with the music, though, start trying to work out tunes by ear.

Remember that written music is only half the story (if that) when it comes to performing music.

46

Every sharp/flat note has two names. F# (F sharp) can also be called G♭ (G flat) – they are the same note. The reason why one name is used instead of another depends on the musical context. F# is said to be the enharmonic equivalent of G♭, E♭ the enharmonic equivalent of D#, and so on. See below:

Table of enharmonic equivalents		
G# (G sharp)	is the same note as	A♭ (A flat)
A#	is the same note as	B♭
C#	is the same note as	D♭
D#	is the same note as	E♭
F#	is the same note as	G♭
Less common equivalents		
E#	is the same note as	F
F♭	is the same note as	E
B#	is the same note as	C
C♭	is the same note as	B

47

The distance between one note and the next note with the same name is an **octave**. For example, the distance between G on the D string, and G on the E string is one octave – the former being one octave lower than the latter. A on the E string is one octave higher than A on the A string. G on the G string is two octaves lower than G on the E string.

48

Playing every note over a single octave will give you a **chromatic scale**. Start and finish on E and you will have the E chromatic scale, start and finish on B♭ (B flat) and you will have the B♭ chromatic scale.

To hear the chromatic scale, play an open string and then each fret of that string up to the 12th. If you do this on the D string, you will hear the twelve notes of the D chromatic scale (thirteen if you include the D on the twelfth fret).

49

The notes of the major scale are taken from the chromatic scale (*described in tip 48*). The example below shows the chromatic scale of D on the D string, from which the D major scale can be extracted. For this example, the most common note names are given, rather than all enharmonic equivalents (*see tip 46*):

Fret	Chromatic scale	Major Scale	
Open	D	D	
1st	E♭		T
2nd	E	E	
3rd	F		T
4th	F♯	F♯	
5th	G	G	S
6th	G♯		T
7th	A	A	
8th	B♭		T
9th	B	B	
10th	C		T
11th	C♯	C♯	
12th	D	D	S

Some notes in the major scale have a gap of two frets, some one. A gap of two frets is known musically as a tone, a gap of one is known as a semitone.

2 frets = Tone (T)
1 fret = Semitone (S)

50

The major scale is worked out using the formula below (T=Tone, S=Semitone):

T - T - S - T - T - T - S

Use this formula and you will arrive at the major scale for whichever note you start on. For example, start on E♭ – apply the formula – get the E♭ major scale

Eb – F – G – Ab – Bb – C – D - Eb

Start on G – apply the formula – get the G major scale

G – A – B – C – D – E – F# - G

See tip 56 on which scales have sharps and which have flats.

51

The formula for the natural minor scale is:

T - S - T - T - S - T - T

Use this formula and you will arrive at the minor scale for the note you started on. For example, start on C – apply the formula – get the C natural minor scale

C – D – Eb – F – G – Ab – Bb - C

Start on B – apply the formula – get the B natural minor scale

B – C# - D – E – F# - G – A - B

See tip 56 on which scales have sharps and which have flats.

52

The basic blues scale is made up of five notes (it is also known as the pentatonic scale). The formula for working out a blues scale is

(T+S) – T – T – (T+S) – T

Use this formula and you will arrive at the blues scale for the note you started on.

E – G – A – B – D – E
A – C – D – E – G – A

53

Here are some more formulas to try out:

T – S – T – T – T – S – T	-	Dorian Mode*
S – T – T – T – S – T – T	-	Phrygian Mode
T – T – T – S – T – T – S	-	Lydian Mode
T – T – S – T – T – S – T	-	Mixolydian Mode

For example, start with E and apply the formula for the Dorian mode, and you will arrive at the E dorian scale. Start with B♭, use the formula for the Mixolydian mode and you will arrive at the B♭ mixolyian mode

* A **mode** is a type of scale. The major and natural minor scales are also known as Ionian and Aeolian modes, respectively.

Try transposing tunes you know well to different keys to get a fresh perspective on them. By doing so, you will also be improving your overall knowledge of the instrument. Try the examples below. Notice how different the two versions of each example feel and sound:

Unusual time-signatures such as 7/8 and 11/8 are easier to get the feel of if broken up into smaller chunks. For example 7/8 (7 eighth-beats) could be split into 4+3 eighth-beats and counted as:

1, 2, 3, 4, 1, 2, 3
1, 2, 3, 4, 1, 2, 3

(the first beat shown in bold) or 3+4 and counted as

1, 2, 3, 1, 2, 3, 4
1, 2, 3, 1, 2, 3, 4

11/8 is normally split into 4+3+4:

1, 2, 3, 4, 1, 2, 3, 1, 2, 3, 4
1, 2, 3, 4, 1, 2, 3, 1, 2, 3, 4

56

Below is a table showing which keys have sharps or flats, and how many they have. Neither C nor A minor (Am) have any sharps or flats, but both A and F sharp minor (F$\sharp$m) have 3 sharps, for example. Because G and Em have the same key signature (number of sharps or flats), they are related. G is the relative major of Em, and Em is the relative minor of G.

Key	Number of sharps or flats in key				
C/Am	No sharps or flats				
G/Em	F$\sharp$				
D/Bm	F$\sharp$	C$\sharp$			
A/F$\sharp$m	F$\sharp$	C$\sharp$	G$\sharp$		
E/C$\sharp$m	F$\sharp$	C$\sharp$	G$\sharp$	D$\sharp$	
F/Dm	B$\flat$				
B$\flat$/Gm	B$\flat$	E$\flat$			
E$\flat$/Cm	B$\flat$	E$\flat$	A$\flat$		
A$\flat$/Fm	B$\flat$	E$\flat$	A$\flat$	D$\flat$	

TRADITIONAL MUSIC

57

Traditional music has always been learned best by ear. To learn a traditional style successfully, it is vital to listen to as much as possible, whether this is through playing with friends, going to gigs or listening to recordings.

58

Popular or traditional tunes will stick in the memory better if they have been learned by ear, rather than from written music. Some written music may be of help if a style is unfamiliar but should not be relied upon too much.

59

Don't rely too much on tune names – there are countless instances of tunes sharing the same name or a single tune having several names.

60

If you play traditional music, don't stick with just a single version of a tune you play – whether it was learned from a friend, off an album or from a collection. The source you have learned from is just another person's version of that tune. Feel free to experiment with the music yourself while still retaining the essential character of the tune.

61

Sometimes it may be difficult to accommodate intricate ornamentation within a tune that is played at speed. Never allow this to detract from the natural flow of the tune. Rather leave out the ornaments.

It can be very effective in 6/8 tunes to shift the
emphasis from the usual 1st and 4th beats of the bar…

…to the 3rd and 6th beats:

this variation should not be overused, however.
Occasional use will be more effective.

63

When learning a traditional style of music, it is always
better to try and copy the sound you hear. If using
written music, remember that it is just a guide. The
subtleties of the style will be easier to pick up by ear.
Think how a child learns to speak its native language –
through listening and copying. Reading comes later.
The process of learning to play traditional music is very
similar.

64

If learning a tune from a collection, bear in mind that
the tune you are looking at is only one player's version
of the tune. It is not the "right" version of the tune –
no such thing exists with traditional music. So use the
written music as a guide, pick up ideas from it (as well
as from other sources), and develop your own version
of the tune.

65

Ornaments and embellishments play an important role, especially in traditional music. They are, however of secondary importance to a tune. They serve to decorate. In the same way, an ornament on the mantelpiece is not part of the structure of the room, it is an addition that should enhance the surroundings. If the room is in a state, or maybe even half-built, then the ornament will serve no purpose.

66

If a tune is losing impetus in a particular section because of a difficult ornament then take it out. Simplify the difficult passage and reinsert the ornament at a later date when you have the basic tune under your fingers. Attempts at difficult ornamentation (triplets, turns etc) should not detract from the tune.

67

Great mandolin players will also be natural improvisers. The selection of tunes that they know will grow organically, unlike a static repertoire of "pieces". They will change over time, as the player's style develops. Take steps to achieve this by not sticking slavishly to a particular version of a tune. Allow variations to appear in your playing.

68

Set aside some time in practice sessions to just experiment. Feel free to make discordant, strange sounds in your search for something beautiful or interesting. Experimentation is the foundation of the exciting world of improvisation and composition.

69

Once you have spent some time improvising, have come up with some good ideas and can write them down, you have moved into the realms of composition. Everyone is capable of creating and, if you can play an instrument, then you are capable of composing. Many are daunted by the word "composer", however. The word conjures up pictures of untouchable geniuses such as Beethoven and Mozart. Remember, though, that one does not have to be Beethoven in order to compose.

70

Improvisation is not a skill that just a small, gifted minority are born with. It takes work and lots of patience. First attempts in improvisation are bound to seem unsure and lacking in confidence, just as first attempts at playing the trumpet, driving a car or baking bread will. Practicing this skill will result in a more assured and natural command of the music.

71

If improvising a solo over a backing or accompaniment, remember that pauses say as much as fast runs of notes. A balance of fast notes, slow notes and pauses will make for a more interesting solo.

72

If improvising a solo within a song, there are two possible approaches:

- Use the key of the song as a starting point. For example, if the song is in D major, start by exploring the D major scale. If the song has a bluesy feel and is in E, start by exploring the E blues scale (*see tips 50-52*). Look out for key changes in the song. A chorus can often be in a different key to the verses.

- Use the melody of the song as a starting point. Play the main melody of the song and add extra notes/ornaments to it from the chosen scale.

Using elements of the song melody along with other ideas taken from the scale will make for an interesting, balanced solo.

73

If a run of notes works particularly well in a solo, do not be afraid to repeat it straight away, or draw on it later on in your solo. A solo with no repetition can appear aimless and laboured.

74

Notes outside the scale of a song or accompaniment can also be very effective if used sparingly in a solo. These sort of notes need to sound like they were intended, rather than accidental.

75

If a discordant note is hit when performing a solo, don't think of it as a mistake. Instead, use it as an opportunity to resolve the note up or down to a note that does work.

76

Many solos use the *question and answer* technique, or *statement and reply*. Think of a run of notes as a short phrase or statement, and the next run of notes as a reply. Do this a few times and you will have a dialogue or conversation. The statements and replies can be long or short, said quickly or meditatively

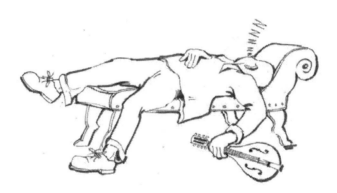

77

Ensure there is a minimum of tension in your body when playing either seated or standing. Common areas to watch out for include:

- **shoulders** – these should not be hunched over. Try to keep them as relaxed as possible.

- **back** – make sure it is straight, whether seated or standing. Ask someone to watch you playing.

- **arms** – these should be relaxed and not forced into position. Any tightness or rigidity will hinder flow of music and cause discomfort.

- **hands** – not gripping too tightly, whether it's the fret-board or the pick.

- **fingers** – avoid unnecessary movement or gripping too hard in the left hand.

78

If you play standing, make sure the mandolin strap is adjusted to a comfortable height. Ideally, your arms should not have to stretch any more or less than if you were playing seated.

79

Remember to keep the mandolin upright, and not angled in such a way to make it easier to see what your fingers are doing. It is common for beginners to do this. Stopping this habit is important, though, as the player should learn to trust their sense of touch rather than sight.

80

It is not uncommon for a player's posture to alter when playing very fast or intensely. This is fine, so long as the body is still relaxed. Keep a look out for extra tension when playing in this way.

81

Know your mandolin. Below is a picture showing the various parts of a flat-back mandolin – the variety that is preferred by traditional and popular music players.

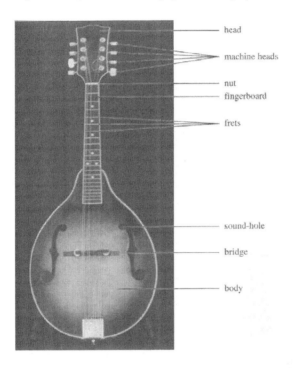

- head
- machine heads
- nut
- fingerboard
- frets
- sound-hole
- bridge
- body

82

If you've bought a second-hand instrument, have it checked/set up by a repairer. It is likely that there will be some minor alterations required.

83

If you see small dents appearing on the frets of your mandolin, just under the strings, then this is a sign of wear. It would be advisable to take your mandolin to a repairer to rectify this.

84

Get your mandolin serviced every now and then by a good repairer – machine heads may start to work less effectively, the bridge may need adjusting, etc. A regular service will lengthen the life of your instrument and keep it in good playing order.

85

Keep your strings clean. A quick wipe along their length with a clean cloth after playing will lengthen their life and keep them sounding sharp.

86

Change strings regularly – the improvement to the sound will be great. Old strings sound lifeless and dull.

87

If you take your mandolin on an aeroplane, take it as hand luggage. If this is not possible, be aware that the strings must be loosened as the pressurised atmosphere in the hold of a plane will increase the string tension. If the strings are not loosened first, this could lead to serious damage.

88

Make sure your gig bag contains clothes pegs. They are invaluable for holding music/set lists down on a stand when playing out doors! There's nothing more embarrassing, when gigging, to have to halt your playing to chase a piece of paper in front of everyone. While you're at it, put some mosquito repellent in there, too. When playing outdoors you are powerless against these dreaded creatures.

89

Mysterious buzzing sounds are a common problem with mandolins. They often occur as a result of something quite harmless:

- Check the machine heads for loose screws.
- Check that loose string ends are not vibrating against machine heads or the head of the mandolin.
- It may be a button/belt buckle or some other object that is attached to your clothing.
- The bridge may be set too low, making the strings vibrate against the frets.

If none of these solve the problem, it may be something more serious.

- The frets may need repairing/replacing
- The neck may be warped/not set up right.
- There may be a crack in the body.

90

Don't become too reliant on electronic tuners– just use them in noisy environments – learn to trust your ear when it comes to tuning up.

91

When buying plectrums, buy as many as you can afford! I have never met a mandolinist who hasn't experienced regular and heavy plectrum loss from the day they bought their very first.

92

Try different thicknesses of plectrum or pick. Thicker plectrums can be great for getting more volume, while thinner picks may be more suitable for faster playing. It is worth experimenting with the wide variety of materials and thicknesses on offer.

93

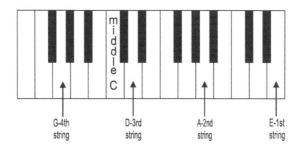

G-4th
string

D-3rd
string

A-2nd
string

E-1st
string

If using a keyboard or piano to tune up, use the notes shown above to give you correct pitches for the mandolin strings. Middle C is the C note found in the middle of the keyboard.

94

When performing in front of an audience, keep in mind that you are your own most scathing critic. Nobody else listens to your playing as critically as you do. Most people are impressed by the fact that you are able to get up and play in front of people at all!

95

Playing with other musicians and along with recordings is a great way to really move forward with any instrument.

96

It is possible to learn a great deal by recording yourself and playing along.

If you have the means, try recording a chord progression over and over. Then listen back and play along, either with a melody part or improvising.

97

Other musicians can be a great source of new ideas, advice and criticism. Always take advice graciously, and make your own informed opinion from the various sources you have around you, whether they be other musicians, teachers, recordings or books.

98

When playing with others, always keep an ear on what they are playing. Find a good balance between concentrating on what you are doing and listening to what others are doing. Disappearing into your own world will weaken the sound of the group.

99

Other instruments in the mandolin family are the mandola, mandocello and mandobass. Along with the mandolin, these correspond with the bowed strings – violin, viola, violoncello and double bass.

100

It is easier to tune *up* an out-of-tune string. That is, when it is lower than the desired pitch. If a string is out of tune, make it lower (even if it is higher) and then tune it up.

101

To play harmonic notes, place the finger directly over the fret – 12th, 7th and 5th are the best – without pressing down. Play the string and immediately remove the left hand. After playing the string, remove the finger immediately to allow the string to vibrate freely.

Printed in Great Britain
by Amazon